The story of the Texas Borderline

Understanding the immigration discussion

Riley Harper

Table of Contents

Introduction

The Texas border crisis has emerged as a focal point of contention between state and federal authorities, with implications for immigration policy, law enforcement, and constitutional principles. By examining the events leading up to the conflict, including the installation of razor wire and fencing by Texas authorities and subsequent clashes with federal agents, this sets the stage for a comprehensive exploration of the multifaceted issues at play. Through a detailed analysis of the evolving situation, this book provides readers with the context and understanding necessary to navigate the complexities of the Texas border crisis.

Setting the Stage for Understanding the Texas Border Crisis

The Texas border crisis unfolds against a backdrop of escalating tensions between state and federal authorities over immigration enforcement policies. It began with Texas authorities taking drastic measures to curb what they perceived as a surge in illegal immigration, particularly along the Texas-Mexico border. This included the installation of razor wire, fencing, and gates in areas like Shelby Park, effectively blocking access for US Border Patrol agents.

The conflict intensified as Texas Governor Greg Abbott asserted the state's right to defend itself from what he termed an "invasion" of migrants. Abbott's actions highlighted the growing rift between state and federal governments on matters of immigration policy and enforcement. Despite legal challenges and Supreme Court rulings, Texas remained steadfast in its efforts to assert control over the border region, leading to a standoff with federal authorities.

The situation reached a critical juncture when tragic events, such as the drowning deaths of migrants near Shelby Park, highlighted the human toll of the crisis. Federal agencies accused Texas of obstructing rescue efforts and aggravating the dangers faced by migrants seeking to cross the border. Meanwhile, Texas officials defended their actions as necessary measures to protect the state's sovereignty and security.

As the Texas border crisis continues to unfold, it underscores broader debates about immigration, federalism, and constitutional authority. Understanding the complexities and dynamics of this crisis requires a nuanced examination of the political, legal, and humanitarian dimensions at play. Through comprehensive analysis and exploration, this book aims to provide readers with insights into the factors shaping the Texas border crisis and its implications for immigration policy and governance.

Chapter 1: The Texas Border Crisis: Background and Context

Historical Overview of Border Policies

Over the years, the border between the United States and Mexico has been a focal point for various immigration policies and enforcement strategies. These policies have evolved in response to changing migration patterns, political dynamics, and security concerns.

One notable aspect highlighted is the implementation of Operation Lone Star by

Texas officials. This state-led initiative represents a significant departure from previous approaches to border enforcement. Operation Lone Star involves deploying Texas National Guard members and implementing aggressive measures, such as erecting razor wire and deploying military personnel along the border.

Additionally, the role of federal agencies, such as Customs and Border Protection (CBP), in border enforcement efforts also come into play. Federal authorities have historically played a central role in shaping immigration policies and coordinating border security operations. However, the emergence of Operation Lone Star has created tensions between Texas and federal agencies, leading to legal disputes and constitutional challenges over jurisdiction and authority.

Overall, these policies highlight the complex and contentious nature of border policies in the United States. It highlights the evolving dynamics between state and federal authorities and the challenges associated with balancing security concerns, humanitarian considerations, and legal obligations.

Escalation of Tensions: Operation Lone Star

Operation Lone Star, a state-led border enforcement program initiated by Texas Governor Greg Abbott, represents a significant departure from previous approaches to border security. The operation aims to address perceived challenges and inadequacies in federal immigration policies, responding to what state officials characterize as a surge in illegal immigration along the Texas-Mexico border. Its objectives include deterring unauthorized crossings, disrupting human trafficking networks, and enhancing security measures to protect border communities.

Under Operation Lone Star, Texas authorities mobilize a range of resources to bolster border security efforts. This includes deploying National Guard troops, law enforcement personnel, and surveillance technology to strategic locations along the border. Additionally, aggressive tactics are employed, such as erecting razor wire, installing barriers, and using riot shields to push migrants back along the Rio Grande riverbank. Saw-bladed buoy barriers have also been installed in the river as part of the operation's escalation of measures.

However, Operation Lone Star has sparked legal and constitutional challenges, particularly regarding jurisdictional issues and conflicts with federal immigration policies. Texas' aggressive enforcement actions have clashed with federal authorities' jurisdiction over immigration enforcement and border security, leading to legal disputes and constitutional questions.

Critics of Operation Lone Star raise humanitarian concerns about its potential consequences. They highlight the risk of injury or harm to migrants, violations of individuals' rights, and challenges in providing aid and assistance, particularly in emergency situations such as drownings or medical emergencies. The operation's aggressive tactics have raised questions about the balance between enforcement measures and humanitarian considerations.

Overall, Operation Lone Star is a controversial and multifaceted border enforcement initiative characterized by tensions between state and federal authorities, legal disputes, and humanitarian considerations. It reflects broader debates and challenges surrounding immigration policy, border security, and the delicate balance between enforcement measures and humanitarian concerns.

Chapter 2: Legal and Constitutional Implications

State vs. Federal Authority: Clash Over Border Enforcement

The clash between state and federal authorities over border enforcement, particularly exemplified by Texas' Operation Lone Star, highlights complex jurisdictional issues and tensions in immigration policy. Texas Governor Greg Abbott's assertion of state authority to address what he perceives as an "invasion" along the Texas-Mexico border has sparked a significant legal and constitutional debate.

At the heart of the conflict is the question of whether states have the authority to unilaterally implement border enforcement measures that may conflict with federal immigration policies and priorities. Governor Abbott argues that Texas has the constitutional right to defend itself from perceived threats and to take action to secure its border, asserting that state authority supersedes federal statutes in this regard.

However, the federal government maintains primary authority over immigration policy and enforcement, as established by the U.S. Constitution and upheld in numerous

Supreme Court decisions. Federal agencies such as Customs and Border Protection (CBP) and Immigration and Customs Enforcement (ICE) are responsible for implementing and enforcing federal immigration laws.

The clash over authority has manifested in various ways, including legal disputes, conflicts over access to border areas, and disagreements over the use of enforcement tactics. For example, Texas' installation of razor wire and barriers along the border has been challenged by federal authorities, leading to court battles and Supreme Court rulings.

Furthermore, conflicts over access to border areas, such as the dispute over Shelby Park in Eagle Pass, Texas, have escalated tensions between state and federal officials. Texas authorities' efforts to block federal Border Patrol agents from accessing certain areas have resulted in confrontations and legal challenges.

The clash over border enforcement authority also reflects broader political and ideological divisions regarding immigration policy. While some state leaders, particularly Republican governors, support Texas' assertive approach to border security, others, including the Biden administration and Democratic officials, emphasize the need for comprehensive federal immigration reform and cooperation between state and federal authorities.

Overall, the state vs. federal authority clash over border enforcement shows the complexities and challenges inherent in immigration policy and enforcement. It raises fundamental questions about the balance of power between state and federal governments, the interpretation of constitutional principles, and the coordination of efforts to address border security and immigration issues.

Supreme Court Intervention: Implications for State and Federal Powers

The Supreme Court intervened in the Texas border crisis by issuing a ruling that allowed federal Border Patrol agents to remove razor wire barriers installed by Texas authorities along the Texas-Mexico border. This intervention followed legal disputes between Texas and federal authorities over jurisdiction and enforcement measures in immigration enforcement.

The legal battle began when Texas implemented Operation Lone Star and installed razor wire along the border as part of its efforts to control immigration. Federal authorities challenged the legality of these measures, arguing that they interfered with federal immigration enforcement and violated federal law.

Texas had previously sued to stop Border Patrol agents from cutting the razor wire, claiming that it illegally destroyed state property and undermined security. However, the Supreme Court's ruling sided with the federal government, granting it the authority to remove the razor wire barriers.

The Supreme Court's decision was significant because it upheld the supremacy of federal immigration law and enforcement authority over conflicting state actions. It clarified the boundaries of state autonomy in border security matters and reinforced the concept of federal preemption, which holds that federal law supersedes conflicting state laws or actions.

Overall, the Supreme Court's intervention resolved a key legal dispute in the Texas border crisis and established important precedents regarding the balance of powers between state and federal authorities in immigration enforcement.

The Supreme Court's intervention in the Texas border crisis revolved around crucial legal disputes and constitutional questions concerning the balance of powers between state and federal authorities in immigration enforcement. At the heart of the legal disputes were conflicts over jurisdiction, enforcement measures, and access to border areas. Texas had implemented Operation Lone Star and installed razor wire along the Texas-Mexico border as part of its efforts to control immigration. However, federal authorities challenged the legality of these measures, leading to legal battles that culminated in the Supreme Court's intervention.

One significant aspect of the Supreme Court's intervention was its ruling allowing federal Border Patrol agents to remove the razor wire barriers installed by Texas authorities. This ruling had implications for state powers, particularly in the realm of border enforcement. It emphasized the supremacy of federal immigration law and enforcement authority, limiting the extent to which states can independently implement border security measures that conflict with federal policy.

Central to the Supreme Court's intervention was the concept of federal preemption, which holds that federal law supersedes conflicting state laws or actions. By allowing federal authorities to remove Texas' razor wire barriers, the Court upheld the principle of federal preemption in immigration enforcement. This decision reinforced the idea that states cannot obstruct or impede federal immigration efforts and clarified the boundaries of state autonomy in border security matters.

The Supreme Court's intervention also highlighted the delicate balance of powers between state and federal governments in immigration and border security. While states retain some authority to address local concerns related to immigration, the Court's ruling emphasized the overarching authority of the federal government in setting and enforcing immigration policy. This decision may establish legal precedent for future conflicts between state and federal authorities over immigration enforcement, shaping the interpretation of constitutional principles and the resolution of similar disputes.

Chapter 3: Human Rights Concerns and Impacts

Violations at the Border: Risks to Immigrants and Border Residents

The violations and risks were faced by both immigrants and border residents amid the Texas border crisis. One significant aspect highlighted was the implementation of Operation Lone Star, a border deterrence program by Texas authorities. The operation involved extreme measures such as the installation of razor wire, fencing, and barricades along the Texas-Mexico border. Despite claims of enhancing security, these measures led to deadly outcomes and endangered the lives of migrants and residents alike.

A pivotal event occurred when Texas authorities seized Shelby Park, effectively blocking federal Border Patrol agents from accessing the area. This obstruction impeded rescue operations and contributed to the tragic drowning of three migrants, including two children, in the nearby Rio Grande. The incident exposed the dire consequences of escalating tensions between state and federal authorities over border enforcement.

Governor Greg Abbott's remarks further exacerbated the situation, with statements suggesting the possibility of shooting migrants and asserting Texas' right to self-defense against perceived invasion. This heightened tensions and raised concerns about potential rights violations and excessive use of force against migrants.

Moreover, the implementation of harsh state laws, including SB 4, authorized state and local police to arrest migrants for improper entry or re-entry. These laws not only increased the likelihood of racial profiling and civil rights abuses but also diverted law enforcement resources away from other public safety concerns, increasing the challenges faced by border communities.

The construction of additional barriers along the border, funded by Texas and totaling billions of dollars, further complicated the situation. Despite claims of enhancing security, these barriers failed to address the root causes of migration and instead contributed to the proliferation of illicit smuggling routes. As a result, migrants were exposed to greater dangers, including exploitation by criminal networks and perilous journeys through remote and deadly terrain.

Border residents along the Texas-Mexico border face significant implications due to border violations. The heightened militarization and surveillance in border areas disrupt daily life for residents, impacting their mobility, access to services, and overall sense of security. Economic repercussions are also evident, with trade disruptions, restrictions on movement, and diversion of resources to border security efforts negatively affecting local businesses and economic development prospects.

Moreover, concerns regarding civil liberties and human rights emerge as residents report incidents of racial profiling, harassment, and excessive use of force by law enforcement agencies. These violations raise fundamental questions about the protection of individual rights and freedoms in border regions. Additionally, the humanitarian impact of border violations is stark, with border communities witnessing firsthand the suffering and tragedy unfolding as migrants and asylum seekers face perilous journeys and encounters with law enforcement.

Community safety is a pressing issue, with risks of violence, crime, and environmental damage associated with illegal border crossings and enforcement operations posing threats to residents' well-being. Despite these challenges, residents, advocacy groups, and civil society organizations work tirelessly to address the needs and rights of border communities. Through advocacy efforts, legal action, and support services, they seek to mitigate the negative impacts of border enforcement while promoting justice, accountability, and dignity for all individuals affected by border policies.

In essence, the implications of border violations exposes the complexity and urgency of addressing border security issues in a holistic manner. A comprehensive approach is necessary, one that recognizes the interconnected social, economic, legal, and humanitarian dimensions of border management while upholding the rights and dignity of all individuals, including both residents and migrants.

Deadly Outcomes: Incidents Involving American Citizens

The latest report from the Texas Department of Public Safety sheds light on the alarming reality of criminal activity perpetrated by illegal aliens in the state. While supporters of illegal immigration often paint migrants as individuals seeking a better life, the report reveals a disturbing pattern of dangerous behavior among some of them.

According to the report, over 573,000 criminal offenses were committed by illegal aliens in Texas over the course of their criminal careers, as documented by the Texas Rangers. This staggering figure is likely just the tip of the iceberg, as it only accounts for state offenses and excludes federal crimes, offenses in other states, and crimes committed by legally present aliens.

Between June 1, 2011, and June 30, 2021, more than 344,000 criminal aliens were booked into local Texas jails, of which over 235,000 were classified as illegal aliens. These individuals were charged with a range of serious offenses, including homicides, assaults, burglaries, drug charges, kidnappings, thefts, robberies, sexual assaults, sexual offenses, obstructing police charges, and weapons charges.

It's important to note that these figures likely underestimate the true extent of criminal activity by illegal aliens, as many individuals evade detection by the Department of Homeland Security (DHS) and are not identified as illegal aliens when arrested for crimes. This underscores the inadequacy of relying solely on encounters with DHS to identify illegal aliens.

The report highlights the failure of policies like "catch and release," which allow illegal aliens to remain in the country despite previous encounters with immigration authorities. The consequence is the victimization of thousands of innocent Texans who would likely still be alive if immigration laws were effectively enforced.

The Texas Department of Public Safety rightly emphasizes that these crimes should never have occurred, and the victims should never have been subjected to such violence. The report underscores the urgent need for securing the border and enforcing immigration laws to protect citizens from preventable harm.

In conclusion, this report serves as a stark reminder of the devastating impact of illegal immigration and the reckless open-border policies of the Biden administration. The safety and security of American citizens must be prioritized through robust border security measures and effective enforcement of immigration laws.

The Escalating Consequences of the Border Crisis

The growing ripple effects of the border crisis are becoming increasingly apparent across various parts of the United States, as reported by Forbes. Local officials in border cities like Laredo, Texas, and Brownsville, Texas, have expressed concerns about the potential inundation of migrants, likening the situation to preparing for a hurricane. Despite expectations of a spike in border crossings after the end of Title 42, the influx of migrants continues to escalate in cities across the country.

In Chicago, Mayor Lori Lightfoot has highlighted the lack of space to accommodate asylum seekers racing to the U.S. border. Similarly, in Washington, D.C., Diana Fula from the Congregation Action Network has raised concerns about the strain on organizations trying to arrange housing and services for migrants bused to the city. Hotels providing temporary shelter are already at full capacity, indicating a looming crisis in the nation's capital.

New York Mayor Eric Adams has proposed housing migrants in a closed Hudson Valley prison, underscoring the desperation to find accommodations for the increasing number of asylum-seekers. The severity of the situation has prompted considerations of housing migrants in unconventional facilities, including a State University of New York campus and a closed correctional facility in Duchess County.

The impact of the border crisis extends beyond humanitarian concerns to affect businesses, particularly in industries reliant on immigrant labor. Bryan Clayton, CEO of

GreenPal, notes the negative repercussions on the landscaping industry, where immigrant workers constitute a significant portion of the workforce. With the surge of migrants at the border, landscape workers face deportation, detention, or exploitation, disrupting businesses and compromising service quality.

In response to the crisis, legislative efforts like the Secure the Border Act of 2023 aim to enhance border security measures, including hiring more Border Patrol agents and resuming border wall construction. However, the bill faces opposition from Democrats and a potential veto from the White House, highlighting the political challenges in addressing the issue.

As an alternative approach, proposals for a guest worker program and pathways to citizenship for undocumented workers offer potential solutions to alleviate pressure on the border and address labor shortages. Implementing these measures could provide legal avenues for migrant workers and mitigate the adverse effects on businesses and communities.

Given the ongoing nature of the border crisis, companies and organizations must proactively assess its potential impact on their operations and update crisis management plans accordingly. By preparing for various scenarios and ensuring access to necessary resources, they can effectively navigate the challenges posed by the evolving border situation.

Chapter 4: Political Responses and Ramifications

Governor Abbott's Stand: Defiance and Support

Governor Abbott took a firm stance on the border crisis, exhibiting both defiance against federal intervention and strong support for Texas' actions. He adamantly argued that Texas possessed the constitutional right to defend itself from what he labeled an "invasion" of illegal immigration. Abbott firmly asserted that this authority "supersedes any federal statutes to the contrary," emphasizing the supremacy of state law in matters of border security.

Despite the Supreme Court's ruling granting the Justice Department's request to remove the state-installed razor wire along the border, Abbott remained resolute in his position. He made it clear that Texas would persist in adding wire along the border, defying the court's decision. Abbott's unwavering stance garnered widespread support from fellow Republican governors across the country, who issued a statement in solidarity with Texas. Notably, former President Donald Trump also voiced his vocal support for Texas' border security measures.

Abbott's defiance against federal intervention reflects his commitment to prioritizing state sovereignty in matters of border enforcement. By challenging federal authority and asserting Texas' right to independently address immigration issues, Abbott positioned himself as a staunch defender of state autonomy. His unwavering stance underscores the deeply contentious nature of the border crisis and the ongoing clash between state and federal authorities over immigration policy and enforcement.

Additionally, Abbott garnered support from other Republican governors across the country, as well as from former President Donald Trump, who also vocalized support for Texas' actions.

National Perspectives: Implications for the Biden Administration and Other States

The Texas border crisis has far-reaching implications for the Biden administration and other states across the nation. The Biden administration faces significant challenges in addressing the crisis, as Texas' defiance and assertiveness in border enforcement highlight broader tensions between state and federal authorities. The implications extend beyond Texas, impacting the Biden administration's immigration policies and its ability to manage border security effectively.

For the Biden administration, the Texas border crisis poses a political and policy dilemma. The administration's approach to immigration and border enforcement has faced scrutiny and criticism, particularly from Republican-led states like Texas. The escalation of tensions with Texas shows the need for the Biden administration to reassess its immigration strategy and address concerns raised by border states regarding border security and immigration enforcement.

Moreover, the crisis in Texas serves as a litmus test for the Biden administration's ability to manage immigration issues and navigate conflicts with states over jurisdictional matters. The administration must balance its commitment to humane immigration policies with the imperative to enforce border security effectively. Failure to effectively address the crisis in Texas could undermine the administration's credibility and impact its broader policy agenda.

Beyond the immediate implications for the Biden administration, the Texas border crisis has reverberations for other states grappling with immigration challenges. The standoff between Texas and the federal government highlights the potential for similar conflicts to arise in other border states, as states assert their authority in immigration enforcement. The outcome of the Texas border crisis will shape the landscape of immigration policy and enforcement nationwide, influencing how other states navigate their own border security priorities.

In conclusion, the Texas border crisis has significant implications for the Biden administration and other states, highlighting the complexities of immigration policy and enforcement at the federal and state levels. Addressing the crisis requires a coordinated approach that balances competing interests and priorities, ensuring effective border security while upholding the principles of fairness and compassion in immigration enforcement.

Chapter 5: Societal and Economic Consequences

Strengthening Illicit Actors: Impact on Criminal Cartels

The Texas border crisis has had a significant impact on criminal cartels, leading to a strengthening of illicit actors in the region. With heightened border tensions and increased security measures, criminal cartels have adapted their tactics to exploit vulnerabilities and capitalize on the chaos.

One of the key ways criminal cartels have benefited from the border crisis is through the smuggling of migrants across the border. As border enforcement efforts intensify, cartels have expanded their human trafficking operations, charging exorbitant fees to migrants seeking entry into the United States. This has resulted in a lucrative source of income for these criminal organizations, further fueling their activities.

Moreover, the diversion of law enforcement resources to address the influx of migrants has created opportunities for criminal cartels to engage in other illicit activities, such as drug trafficking and weapons smuggling. With authorities stretched thin, cartels have exploited gaps in border security to transport drugs and weapons across the border, contributing to the proliferation of illegal substances and firearms in the region.

Additionally, the border crisis has exacerbated existing challenges related to gang violence and organized crime along the border. Criminal cartels have taken advantage of the chaos to expand their influence and control over smuggling routes, leading to increased competition and conflict among rival gangs. This has resulted in heightened levels of violence and insecurity in border communities, posing significant challenges for law enforcement agencies tasked with maintaining public safety.

Overall, the Texas border crisis has provided criminal cartels with opportunities to strengthen their operations and increase their influence in the region. Addressing these challenges will require a coordinated and comprehensive approach that addresses both the root causes of migration and the underlying factors fueling criminal activity along the border.

Public Resources and Policies: Cost of Operation Lone Star

The Operation Lone Star initiative, launched by Texas Governor Greg Abbott, has incurred significant costs to public resources and policies. The comprehensive mobilization of state resources, including the deployment of the Texas National Guard, Border Patrol agents, and additional law enforcement personnel, has necessitated substantial financial investments. These expenses encompass various aspects, such as personnel salaries, equipment procurement, infrastructure development, and operational logistics.

The financial burden of Operation Lone Star extends beyond immediate expenditures to encompass broader economic implications for the state. The allocation of funds towards border security efforts diverts resources from other essential public services and initiatives, potentially impacting areas such as education, healthcare, and infrastructure development. Furthermore, the sustained deployment of state resources to border enforcement activities may strain budgetary allocations over the long term, necessitating careful consideration of fiscal sustainability.

In addition to direct financial costs, Operation Lone Star has implications for public policies and governance frameworks. The initiative represents a significant expansion of state authority and intervention in immigration enforcement, raising questions about the balance of power between state and federal entities. The deployment of military and law enforcement personnel to the border also raises concerns about the militarization of border communities and the potential impact on civil liberties and human rights.

Moreover, the operational approach of Operation Lone Star, characterized by heightened surveillance, border fortifications, and law enforcement activities, may have broader societal implications. The emphasis on deterrence and enforcement measures may contribute to a climate of fear and mistrust within border communities, affecting social cohesion and community relations. Additionally, the diversion of resources towards enforcement-focused strategies may detract from holistic approaches to addressing the root causes of migration and promoting regional stability.

Overall, the cost of Operation Lone Star extends beyond financial expenditures to Include broader implications for public resources, policies, and societal dynamics. As policymakers evaluate the effectiveness and sustainability of border security initiatives, careful consideration of these multifaceted impacts is essential to ensure that public resources are effectively allocated and policies align with broader societal goals and values.

Chapter 6: Future Prospects and Resolutions

Pathways to Resolution: Legal, Political, and Diplomatic Efforts

The resolution of the Texas border crisis involves a Multi-dimensional approach encompassing legal, political, and diplomatic efforts aimed at addressing the underlying issues and resolving tensions between state and federal authorities. From a legal perspective, both Texas and the federal government are pursuing various avenues to assert their respective authorities and challenge actions taken by the opposing party. Texas has invoked state law and constitutional arguments to defend its actions, particularly Governor Abbott's assertion of the state's right to defend itself against what it perceives as an "invasion" at the border. Conversely, the federal government has utilized the judiciary system to challenge Texas' actions, seeking court orders to remove state-installed barriers and assert federal authority over immigration enforcement.

On the political front, this plays a significant role in shaping public perception and influencing the trajectory of the crisis. Texas Governor Greg Abbott and other Republican leaders have framed the issue as a matter of state sovereignty and national security, garnering support from fellow Republicans and former President Donald Trump. In contrast, the Biden administration and Democratic officials emphasize the need for federal oversight and cooperation to effectively address immigration challenges.

Diplomatic engagement is also crucial, considering the implications of the border crisis beyond domestic policy. Diplomatic channels are utilized to address cross-border issues such as migrant flows, border security cooperation, and the implications of unilateral actions taken by Texas on international relations. Dialogue and negotiation with Mexico are particularly important to manage the flow of migrants, address humanitarian concerns, and maintain diplomatic relations amid tensions at the border.

In conclusion, a comprehensive approach that combines legal, political, and diplomatic efforts is necessary to navigate the complexities of the Texas border crisis. Balancing state autonomy with federal authority while addressing underlying immigration challenges requires collaboration and cooperation across multiple levels of government and with international partners.

Long-Term Solutions: Addressing Root Causes and Building Cooperation

Addressing the root causes and building cooperation are essential components of long-term solutions to the Texas border crisis. Recognizing that the surge in migrant crossings is symptomatic of broader issues, efforts are directed towards addressing underlying factors that drive migration and fostering cooperation among stakeholders.

One aspect of long-term solutions involves addressing the root causes of migration, including poverty, violence, and lack of economic opportunity in countries of origin. By investing in development programs, job creation initiatives, and governance reforms, policymakers aim to tackle the systemic issues that drive people to migrate. Collaborative efforts with international partners, including Central American governments and regional organizations, are crucial to implementing effective strategies that address root causes and create sustainable alternatives to migration.

Additionally, building cooperation among federal, state, and local authorities, as well as international partners, is essential for effective border management and immigration enforcement. Coordination mechanisms, information-sharing protocols, and joint operations help streamline efforts to secure the border, combat human trafficking, and address humanitarian challenges. Moreover, fostering partnerships with non-governmental organizations, community groups, and civil society organizations strengthens support systems for legal migrants and facilitates their integration into host communities.

Furthermore, long-term solutions require comprehensive immigration reform that addresses legal pathways for migration, asylum processes, and border security measures. By modernizing immigration laws and policies, policymakers seek to create a more orderly and humane system that balances enforcement with compassion and respects the rights of migrants.

Overall, addressing the root causes of migration, fostering cooperation among stakeholders, and implementing comprehensive immigration reform are integral to achieving long-term solutions to the Texas border crisis. By tackling underlying issues, enhancing collaboration, and enacting meaningful policy reforms, stakeholders can work towards a more sustainable and equitable approach to managing migration and border security.

Chapter 7: Supreme Court Approval

The Supreme Court decision: Texas approved to enforce its controversial immigration law

The Supreme Court's decision on Tuesday, March 19, 2024, has paved the way for Texas to implement a contentious immigration law, allowing state officials to arrest and detain individuals suspected of entering the country illegally. This move comes despite dissent from the court's three liberal justices.

While legal challenges against the law are ongoing in federal appeals court, the ruling represents a significant albeit temporary victory for Texas in its ongoing immigration policy dispute with the Biden administration.

Senate Bill 4, signed by Texas Governor Greg Abbott in December, immediately sparked concerns among immigration advocates about potential racial profiling and increased detentions and deportation attempts by state authorities, particularly in a state where Latinos make up 40% of the population.

The court's decision, made in response to emergency applications, lacked detailed reasoning. Justice Amy Coney Barrett, in a concurring opinion joined by Justice Brett Kavanaugh, noted that the appeals court had issued only a temporary "administrative" order. Barrett emphasized the court's reluctance to intervene in matters concerning administrative stays pending appeal.

In her dissent, Justice Sonia Sotomayor expressed concern that the order could lead to further chaos and crisis in immigration enforcement. She argued that the law undermines the longstanding federal-state balance of power, granting Texas the authority to enforce criminal penalties on thousands of noncitizens and mandate their removal to Mexico. Sotomayor warned of potential disruptions in foreign relations, hindrance to federal enforcement efforts, and deterrence of noncitizens from reporting abuse or trafficking.

Chapter 8: Conclusion

Reflections on the Texas Border Crisis: Lessons Learned and Paths Forward

Reflecting on the Texas border crisis reveals a complex interplay of legal, political, and humanitarian factors. The crisis has exposed the challenges of balancing state and federal authority in immigration enforcement, as seen in the clash between Texas Governor Greg Abbott and federal authorities over border policies. The Supreme Court's intervention highlighted the tensions between state sovereignty and federal supremacy in matters of immigration law.

One key lesson learned from the crisis is the need for coordinated and cooperative efforts among federal, state, and local authorities to address border security effectively. Operation Lone Star, launched by Governor Abbott, aimed to enhance border enforcement but faced criticism for its impact on border residents and the strained resources it required. The operation highlighted the importance of considering the broader implications of border security measures on communities and public resources.

Moreover, the crisis shed light on the vulnerabilities faced by migrants attempting to cross the border, including the risks of exploitation by criminal cartels and the dangers of the journey itself. The tragic drowning of migrants in the Rio Grande exposed the human cost of border policies and the need for humanitarian responses to border challenges.

Looking forward, addressing the root causes of migration, such as poverty, violence, and lack of opportunity in migrants' home countries, emerges as a crucial long-term solution. Building cooperation with international partners and investing in development aid to address these underlying issues can help reduce the drivers of irregular migration and alleviate pressure on border communities.

In conclusion, the Texas border crisis serves as a sobering reminder of the complex nature of immigration challenges and the need for comprehensive and compassionate approaches to address them. By learning from the lessons of this crisis and embracing cooperation, stakeholders can work towards more effective and sustainable solutions to border security and migration issues.